On the River
ABC

Roberts Rinehart Publishers

A Little Rhino Book

by Caroline Stutson

illustrated by Anna-Maria L. Crum

May your days be filled with wondrous sights and careful consideration for all that you discover.

Dedicated to Sue Enderin, who has shared the mountains and rivers with so many.

— C.S.

To my father, who shared with me his love of literature and Colorado.

— A.L.C.

Copyright © 1993 by Caroline Stutson and Anna-Maria L. Crum

International Standard Book Number 1-879373-46-7
Library of Congress Catalog Card Number 92-061907

Library of Congress Cataloging-in-Publication Data

Stutson, Caroline.
    On the river ABC / by Caroline Stutson ; illustrated by Anna-Maria
Crum.
        p.   cm.
    "A little rhino book."
    Summary: An ant encounters an alphabet of wildlife as it is swept
down a river during a summer storm.
    ISBN 1-879373-46-7 : $12.95
    1. Rivers—Juvenile poetry.   2. Children's poetry, American.
3. Alphabet rhymes. [1. American poetry.   2. Animals—Poetry.
3. Rivers—Poetry.   4. Alphabet.]   I. Crum, Anna-Maria, ill.
II. Title.
PS3569.T88505   1993
811'.54—dc20   92-61907
                                                                         CIP
                                                                          AC

Published in the United States by
Roberts Rinehart Publishers, Post Office Box 666,
Niwot, Colorado 80544

Published in Canada by
Key Porter Books, 70 The Esplanade,
Toronto, Ontario M5E 1R2

Under
the sudden
thunder
of a summer storm,
an Ant spins on her leaf
and tumbles in the
torrent.

By Beaver's pond, upon her boat, she floats.

Beneath the wings
of Cormorant,
she rings
the
shore.

By willow
woods with sleeping Deer
inside. . . .

Through ghostly bogs
where *E*arwigs
hide. . . .

Before the gold
of *F*oxes' eyes. . . .

By pocket Gophers buried deep. . . .

Beyond the reach of *H*eron's beak. . . .

Past  Inchworm

on his stick

adrift. . . .

By ay who calls
to all
to start the day. . . .

Along the bank where Kinglets flit,

then over speckled
pepper
stones,
and on by
Lynx,
she sails
alone.

Between the knees of Moose, she flees. . . .

Near ative trout
in cool, clear
places. . . .

Down
rapid
chutes
in
Ouzel
races. . . .

Past
*P*elican

and rustling
*Q*uail,

beside the
*R*iver otter's
bobbing tail. . . .

By garter Snakes that curve the trail. . . .

By Turtle sunning on his rock. . . .

By Upland plover in a flock. . . .

By ole
who creep in
meadow beds

where proud Wapiti raise their heads. . .

to eXit
on some distant shore
to build her world
anew
once more,

where Yellow warblers circle high
with black wing Zebra butterflies.

Although the river in this story is a mythical one, composed of many rivers like the Colorado, the Snake, the Niobrara, the Green, the Rio Grande, and the Yellowstone, all of the wildlife depicted here is authentic and can be found in the West and the Southwest.

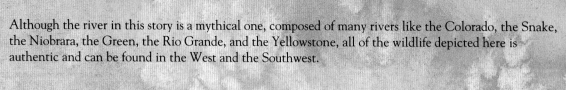

A ... ANT

If you've ever sat down on a RED ANT colony, you will agree that the ant on this river journey was chosen more for her interesting color than for her disposition. It is also true that half of all 10,000 species of ants do sting!

B ... BEAVER

Did you know that BEAVERS, famous for constructing dams, dikes, and lodges, don't always build their homes? On fast moving water, look for a den or burrow in the river bank. It might belong to a beaver.

C ... CORMORANT

Many people think cormorants are sea birds. With their long necks and hooked tip beaks, all cormorants are fishing birds, but only the DOUBLE-CRESTED CORMORANT flies inland to nest.

D ... DEER

The Rocky Mountain region has five habitats for MULE DEER: mountain mahogany and scrub oak; forests of aspen and pine; plains' river beds; and sagebrush mixed with pinyon and juniper. Is it any wonder we see so many deer?

E ... EARWIG

Who'd have thought that EARWIGS would be good mothers? Most insects are long gone by the time their young hatch, but not the earwig! Don't get too close though; those ugly pincers really do pinch!

F ... FOX

The RED FOX, an omnivore, will eat just about anything. In the cover of darkness, he uses his keen sense of smell to dig worms, frogs, insects, lizards, snakes, rabbits, and mice. For dessert; some berries, fruit, and grasses!

G ... GOPHER

NORTHERN POCKET GOPHERS are named for their external cheek pouches, used to carry food. Even when the gopher's mouth is closed, the yellow gnawing teeth remain visible.

H ... HERON

The GREAT BLUE HERON is America's largest wading bird. These magnificent creatures are not endangered, but their wetland habitats are rapidly disappearing.

I ... INCHWORM

The MEASURING WORM has many names: inchworm; span worm; and "looper." By any name, the inchworm, which is really a moth caterpillar, loops along when crawling. That's because there are only two or three pairs of prolegs on the back part of the inchworm's body. Other caterpillars have five.

J ... JAY

If you've ever taken a picnic to the high country, you have probably encountered jays. Although the STELLAR'S JAY, the only western jay with a crest, is a bit shyer than the gray jay, he can be just as persistent. But try to resist his begging, it is better for wild birds to find their own food.

K ... KINGLETS

Although the RUBY-CROWNED KINGLET looks like a perpetual-motion machine with its constantly twitching wings, these tiny birds are most difficult to spot among the evergreens.

L ... LYNX

The yellow-eyed Lynx resembles and is closely related to the bobcat. You can tell them apart by the dark ring covering the end of a lynx's tail. But who would want to get close enough to do that?

M ... MOOSE

Not only the tallest mammal in America, the MOOSE is also the largest antlered animal in the world! Small eyes, huge nose and ears, with a walk that makes you smile; surely somewhere, the screws upon the moose are loose!

N ... NATIVE TROUT

The native trout or CUTTHROAT is easily identified by the vivid red or orange slash under the mouth. These fish and other varieties of trout can be found feeding on freshwater shrimp and insect larvae in our mountain streams and lakes.

O ... OUZEL

Even the roaring rapids can't drown out the music of the OUZEL, America's only aquatic songbird. In search of a tasty bug, the ouzel dips and dives, even running underwater at times.

P ... PELICAN

The goose-sized WHITE PELICAN works in a group to surround and catch fish; the mothers then regurgitate a fishy mixture into their bills for the young. But please keep your distance; visitors have contributed to the high death rate among this threatened species by scaring off the nesting parents.

Q ... QUAIL

It's easy figuring out how the NORTHERN BOBWHITE QUAIL got its name. In the spring when the old covey breaks up, a male quail calls "bob-white" until a female stays to raise a new family. The male also helps rear the offspring, even incubating the eggs, an unusual trait among birds.

R ... RIVER OTTER

Due to unregulated trapping and loss of habitat from water pollution, the river otter was considered endangered. Now, with the release of captive-bred otters, this playful member of the weasel family is slowly spreading out and reproducing in a number of western rivers. Long may they play!

S ... SNAKES

Riparian, or river habitats, are perfect for WANDERING GARTER SNAKES, although they are found away from water too. If you have ever picked one up, you know these snakes expel a nasty smelling liquid when they are frightened!

T ... TURTLE

The SNAPPING TURTLE can weigh up to fifty pounds! With their long necks, these critters can snap from quite a distance if cornered. You can sometimes see them sunning by the water's edge, but mostly snapping turtles like to stay submerged. Ducklings beware!

U ... UPLAND PLOVER

A flock of UPLAND PLOVER makes a pretty picture, but not one you'd usually see on a river. These migratory shorebirds, now called upland sandpipers, were on the decline until a greater understanding of their needs, along with better grasslands management, turned things around.

V ... VOLE

The next time you're hiking, look for areas of clipped grass between the rocks, a sign that the tiny Vole may be nearby.

W ... WAPITI

Along with deer, moose, and caribou, WAPITI, or elk, belong to a family called Cervidae, a group that sheds their antlers every year. In the summer, elk antlers are covered with soft velvet; by fall, they are hard and sharp.

X ... EXIT

To EXIT is to leave. If we care enough about the wildlife on and near our rivers and wetlands, we won't let that happen.

Y ... YELLOW WARBLER

From coast to coast, you can hear the cheerful song of the YELLOW WARBLER. The bird is an optimist! When sneaky cowbirds slip eggs into the yellow warbler's nest, the warbler covers them up and begins again, no matter how long it takes!

Z ... ZEBRA BUTTERFLY

The ZEBRA LONGWING BUTTERFLY lives mainly in the South and Southwest where its plant food, the passion flower, grows. Unlike many other butterflies, the zebra butterfly does not make a tasty mouthful for predators because it feeds on this poisonous flower vine.